THE FOLLOWING KIDISMS
STEM FROM THE MIND OF:

GRACE

· ·

QUOTES & QUESTIONS

a journal for your kid's quotable moments

created & illustrated by
Kate Pocrass

CHRONICLE BOOKS

SAN FRANCISCO

TIONS

Kids ask a lot of questions. The hows and whys come at us all day long.

Now it's time to ask back! The following pages are filled with thoughtful, silly, and technical questions to encourage observation and help kids keep their imagination flowing. What's going on in your child's head is often much more hilarious than you could ever predict. Asking open-ended questions is a fun way to find out how kids interpret the world. Whether you pose these questions to bond over the dinner table or pass the time on a road trip, they will certainly spark some impressive conversations and keep the entire family entertained.

After all, how well do you know what makes your little one tick?

WHICH IS BETTER: DAYTIME OR NIGHTTIME?

Daytime

WHY?   Because I like to
play all the time. I like
playing with balls & dolls,
I guess.

GET TO
MEET A PANDA
SOMEDAY

MORE PLAYING,
LESS SLEEPING

CARNIVAL
COMES TO
TOWN

FIND MISPLACED
TREASURE IN
JACKET POCKET

GOING INTO
SPACE

MAC 'N' CHEESE
FOR LUNCH

WHAT IS YOUR BIGGEST HOPE?

WHAT MAKES A RAINBOW?

The sun because of Jesus
because of His power—
It's RED, yellow, green and
blue and don't forget
purple.
There's two clouds at the
ENDs just for Nice.
There's RAINbows iN the
forest because of Jesus,
He makes everything.

HOW DO CARS WORK?

They have an engine.

I don't know anything about cars, but I do know Jesus makes them.

Feb 2020

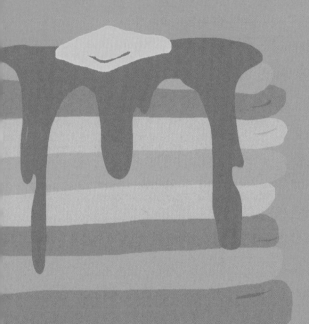

PAJAMA
PANCAKE
SATURDAY

WHAT DO YOU LOOK FORWARD TO ON THE WEEKENDS?

Well, I'll do whatever I want. I go to Sunday school because I like learning about Jesus.

FINALLY
REACHING
THE CEILING

DESCRIBE A PERFECT DAY

My favorite day is Saturday because I like doeing whatever I want like play outside with my yellow & blue ball. I throw it to Rowdy, & he captures it, and he throws it back to me.

UNICYCLE
BASKETBALL

WHAT IS SOMETHING DIFFICULT YOU WOULD LIKE TO LEARN TO DO?

WHAT IS A DREAM?

TiNY HEDGEHOG
THAT LOOKS LIKE
A SCRUB BRUSH

IF YOU COULD HAVE ANY ANIMAL AS A PET, WHAT WOULD IT BE?

WHAT IS YOUR FAVORITE COLOR AND WHY?

HOLD THE OTHER
END OF THE JUMP ROPE

HOW DO YOU MAKE A FRIEND?

spring summer

winter fall

WHY DO WE HAVE DIFFERENT SEASONS?

HOW DO YOU FEEL ABOUT WAKING UP IN THE MORNING?

WHY DO PEOPLE FALL IN LOVE?

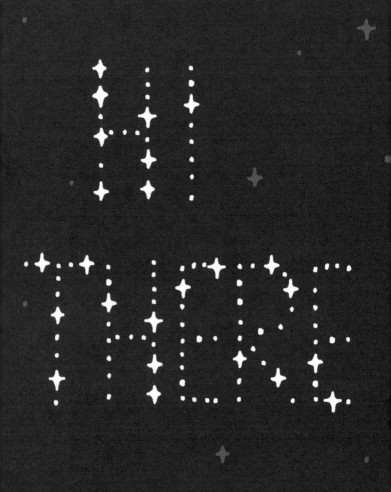

IF YOU MET AN ALIEN, WHAT WOULD YOU SAY TO IT?

invisibility

super
strength

time travel

night vision

telepathy

IF YOU COULD HAVE ANY SUPERPOWER, WHAT WOULD IT BE?

WHEN DO YOU GET BORED?

THE SMELL
OF POPCORN

WHAT MAKES YOU HUNGRY?

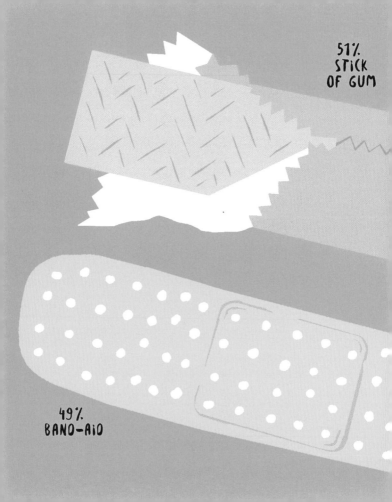

51%
STICK
OF GUM

49%
BAND-AID

WHAT HELPS YOU FELL BETTER WHEN YOU GET HURT?

HOW DO YOU FEEL ABOUT RAIN?

WHERE DOES THE MOON GO WHEN YOU CAN'T SEE IT?

ART
SUPPLIES

WHAT DO YOU WISH YOU HAD MORE OF?

8 SURE-FIRE WAYS TO CURE STUBBORN HICCUPS

GET SCARED

DRINK A SPOONFUL OF VINEGAR

BREATHE INTO A PAPER BAG

TICKLE THE ROOF OF YOUR MOUTH

HOLD YOUR BREATH & SWALLOW THREE TIMES

EAT A TEASPOON OF SUGAR

DRINK WATER UPSIDE DOWN

EAT A BIG GLOB OF PEANUT BUTTER

WHAT ARE HICCUPS?

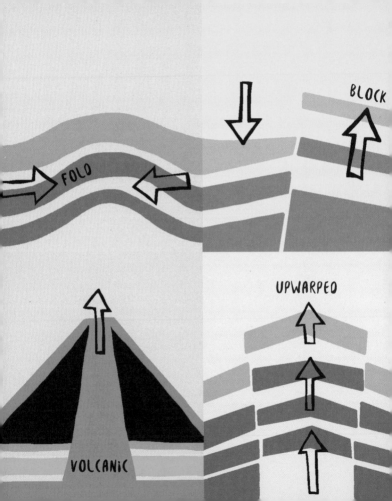

HOW ARE MOUNTAINS FORMED?

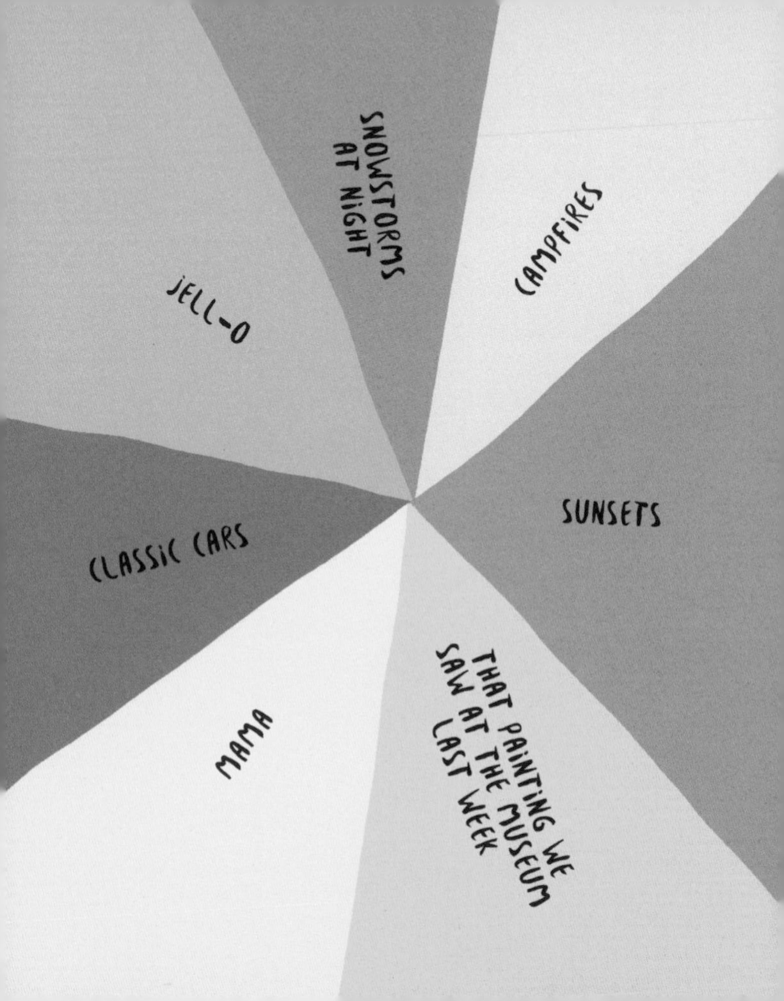
SNOWSTORMS AT NIGHT
CAMPFIRES
JELL-O
SUNSETS
CLASSIC CARS
THAT PAINTING WE SAW AT THE MUSEUM LAST WEEK
MAMA

WHAT IS BEAUTY?

WHICH IS BETTER: CHOCOLATE ICE CREAM OR VANILLA ICE CREAM?

WHY?

DESCRIBE A BRAVE THING YOU'VE DONE

AHHHH
HEE HEE
AGAIN
HEE HEE

WHAT DOES TICKLISH FEEL LIKE?

WHAT DOES THE INTERNET DO?

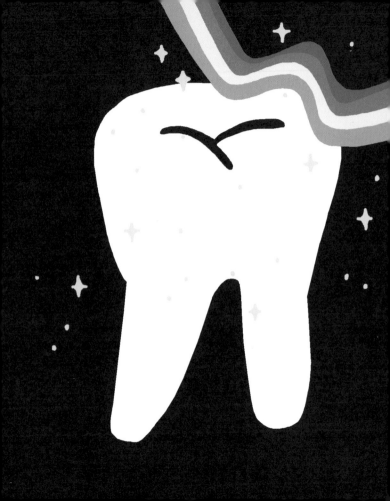

WHAT HAPPENS WHEN YOU LOSE A TOOTH?

I'LL NEVER FORGET THAT TIME WHEN...

WHAT IS A MEMORY?

WOULD YOU RATHER SLEEP IN A TENT OUTSIDE OR A BED INSIDE?

WHY DO ELEPHANTS HAVE TRUNKS?

WHEN IS THE BEST TIME TO DANCE?

....

....

....

....

WITH WHOM?

....

....

....

....

WHY IS THE OCEAN SALTY?

WHAT DOES HAPPINESS FEEL LIKE?

WHY DO FINGERS WRINKLE IN THE BATH?

*1/2 INCH LONG

WHAT IS THE STRONGEST ANIMAL?

LAUGHED SO
HARD THAT i
FARTED

WHAT IS THE SILLIEST THING YOU'VE EVER DONE?

Meeeoo
ooooow
Woooo
ooooof
Meeeow
wooof

WOULD YOU RATHER BE A DOG OR A CAT?

WHY?

TELL ME ABOUT A TIME WHEN YOU FELT SHY

WHAT IS THE COZIEST THING YOU OWN?

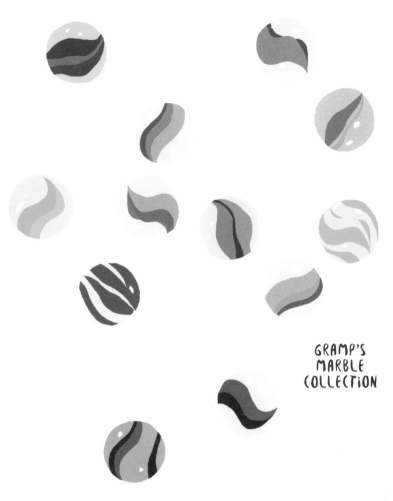

GRAMP'S
MARBLE
COLLECTION

WHAT WOULD YOU HATE TO LOSE?

WHO IS YOUR HERO?

WHY?

LIE IN THE GRASS AND
WATCH THE SUNSET

WHAT IS YOUR FAVORITE THING TO DO WITH YOUR FAMILY?

WOULD YOU RATHER GO SWIMMING ON A HOT DAY OR SLEDDING ON A SNOWY DAY?

brave
silly
loud
friendly
kind

DESCRIBE YOURSELF IN FIVE WORDS

IF YOU WERE GRANTED THREE WISHES, WHAT WOULD THEY BE?

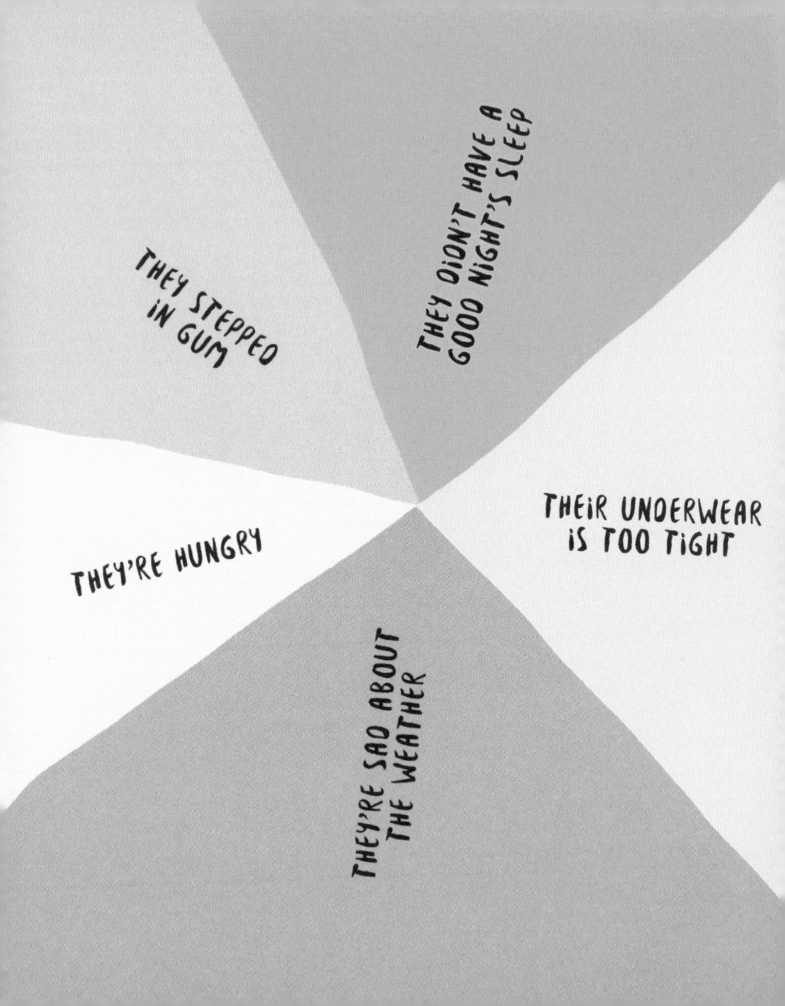
THEY DIDN'T HAVE A GOOD NIGHT'S SLEEP
THEY STEPPED IN GUM
THEIR UNDERWEAR IS TOO TIGHT
THEY'RE HUNGRY
THEY'RE SAD ABOUT THE WEATHER

WHY ARE SOME PEOPLE MEAN?

CLOUDS SNEEZING

WHERE DOES WIND COME FROM?

WHAT IS THE WORST JOB IN THE WORLD?

....

....

....

....

AND THE BEST?

....

....

....

....

HOW DO BEES MAKE HONEY?

WHY CAN'T I
DRAW ON THE WALLS?

WHY DO I HAVE TO
BE A CERTAIN
HEIGHT TO RIDE THE
FERRIS WHEEL?

WHY CAN'T DESSERT
COME BEFORE DINNER?

WHY CAN'T I CLIMB
MY BOOKSHELF?

WHY DO I HAVE TO
WAIT TILL EVERYONE
IS SEATED
BEFORE EATING?

WHY CAN DRIVERS
TURN RIGHT
ON A RED LIGHT?

WHAT RULE DOESN'T MAKE SENSE TO YOU?

.

TALK ABOUT A TIME WHEN SOMEONE MADE YOU FRUSTRATED

running
funning
sunning
punning
stunning
rerunning

WHAT WAS THE BEST PART OF TODAY?

OFFERED MY SEAT
TO SOMONE WHO
NEEDED IT MORE
THAN i DiD

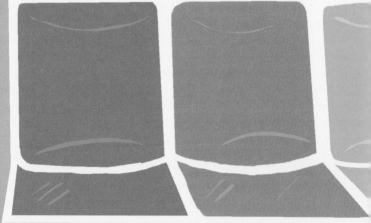

HOW HAVE YOU HELPED SOMEONE RECENTLY?

HOW DOES A CAMERA TAKE PHOTOS?

NAME ONE THING YOU ARE THANKFUL FOR

....

WHY?

....

....

....

....

....

....

....

WHERE DO IDEAS COME FROM?

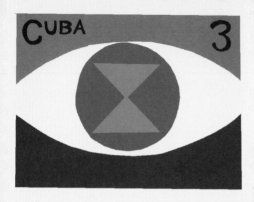

CUBA 3

URUGU

BUL

PAR AVION

nations
unies

70

HOW DOES MAIL WORK?

JAN JUL
FEB AUG
MAR SEP
APR OCT
MAY NOV
JUN DEC

WHAT IS THE BEST MONTH OF THE YEAR?

WE GET THERE
IN A HOT AIR
BALLOON

DESCRIBE YOUR DREAM VACATION

WHAT DOES THE PRESIDENT DO?

WHAT KEEPS THE SUN SHINING?

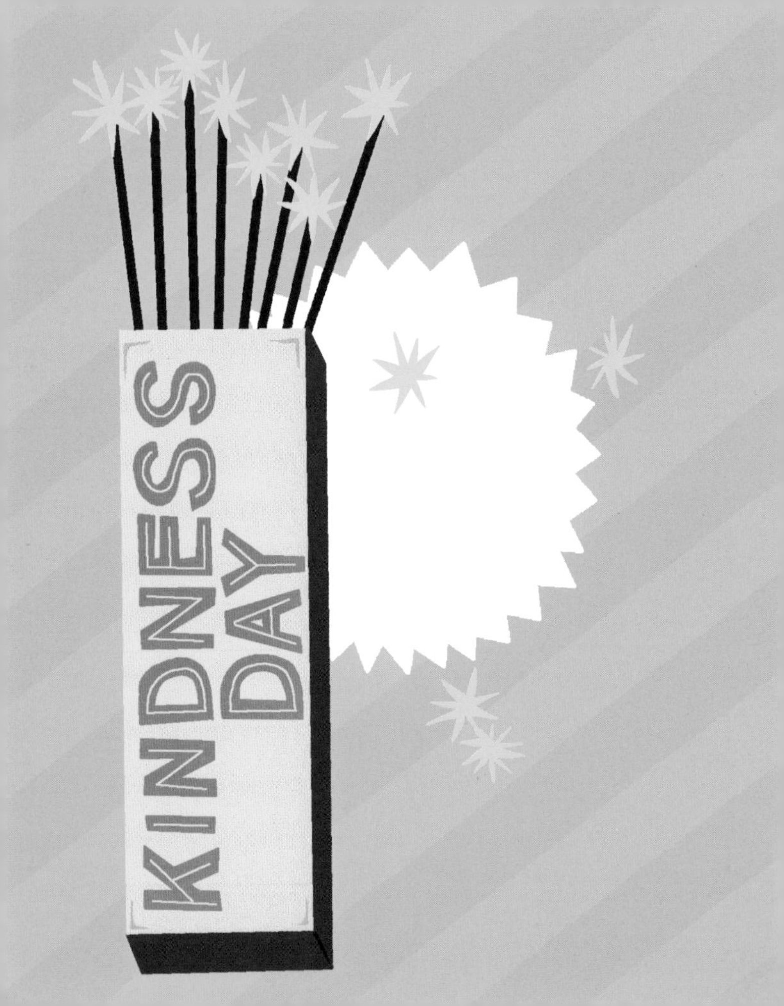
KINDNESS
DAY

IF YOU COULD MAKE UP A NEW HOLIDAY, WHAT WOULD IT BE?

IF YOU MADE YOUR OWN MOVIE, WHAT WOULD YOU CALL IT?

FINDING A
BANANA SLUG
ON MY BANANA

WHAT IS THE MOST DISGUSTING THING YOU CAN THINK OF?

EAT A WHOLE LOT OF ICE CREAM
BUILD INTRICATE LEGO CITIES
SING SONGS & START ROCK BANDS
*FALL ASLEEP WATCHING T.V.
*DO THE DISHES
*USUAL REALITY

WHAT DO ADULTS DO AFTER KIDS GO TO BED?

....

....

....

....

....

....

....

....

....

IF YOU COULD SHRINK DOWN TO THE SIZE OF
AN ANT, WHAT WOULD YOU DO?

WHY DO FLOWERS SMELL?

WHERE DOES YOUR HOME GET ITS WATER FROM?

WHAT DOES YOUR NEIGHBORHOOD LOOK LIKE?

IF YOUR FAVORITE TOY COULD TALK,
WHAT WOULD YOU ASK IT?

i spy
sit
stare
sing
snack
soliloquy

WHAT'S THE BEST WAY TO HAVE FUN ON A ROAD TRIP?

WHO IS THE BEST MUSICIAN IN THE WORLD?

A QUESTION YOU ASKED US:

A QUESTION YOU ASKED US:

A QUESTION YOU ASKED US:

A QUESTION YOU ASKED US:

A QUESTION YOU ASKED US:

A QUESTION YOU ASKED US:

A QUESTION YOU ASKED US:

A QUESTION YOU ASKED US:

They said what?

Is there anything more likely to put a grin on your face than the innocent and insightful remarks of your child? Use the following pages to jot down the hilarious, ingenious, and downright outrageous things your kids say.

No matter how random, these pages will have the whole family laughing for years to come.

AGE: . . . .

PLACE: . . . .

AGE: ....

PLACE: ....

AGE: ....

PLACE: ....

AGE: ....

PLACE: ....

AGE: ....

PLACE: ....

AGE: ....

PLACE: ....

AGE:............................

PLACE:............................

175

AGE: ....

PLACE: ....

AGE: ....

PLACE: ....

AGE: ....
PLACE: ....

AGE:

PLACE:

AGE: ....

PLACE: ....

AGE: ....

PLACE: ....

AGE: ....
PLACE: ....

AGE:

PLACE:

AGE: ....

PLACE: ....

AGE:

PLACE:

AGE:............................

PLACE:...........................

187

AGE: ....

PLACE: ....

AGE: ....

PLACE: ....

AGE: ....
PLACE: ....

AGE:

PLACE:

AGE: ....

PLACE: ....

AGE: ....

PLACE: ....

AGE: ....

PLACE: ....

AGE: ....

PLACE: ....

AGE: ....

PLACE: ....

AGE:

PLACE:

197

AGE:............................

PLACE:............................

AGE: . . . .

PLACE: . . . .

AGE: ....

PLACE: ....

AGE: ....

PLACE: ....

AGE: . . . .

PLACE: . . . .

AGE: ....

PLACE: ....

AGE: ....

PLACE: ....

AGE: ....

PLACE: ....

AGE: ....

PLACE: ....

AGE: ....

PLACE: ....

AGE:
PLACE:

209

AGE:.............................

PLACE:.........................

211

AGE: ....

PLACE: ....

AGE: ....

PLACE: ....

AGE: ....

PLACE: ....

AGE:

PLACE:

AGE: ....

PLACE: ....

AGE: ....

PLACE: ....

ISBN 978-1-4521-7036-7

Manufactured in China

Illustrations and design by Kate Pocrass
See the full range of Kate Pocrass gifts at
www.chroniclebooks.com.

Band-Aid is a registered trademark.
Heinz is a registered trademark.
Jell-O is a registered trademark.

10 9 8 7 6 5 4 3 2 1

Chronicle Books LLC
680 Second Street
San Francisco, California 94107
www.chroniclebooks.com